Introduct

The Shropshire Hills are simply stunn designated 'An Area of Outstanding Natural Beauty'. The main bulk of the higher ground is concentrated upon the wonderful Long Mynd, which provides a backdrop to the pretty town of Church Stretton, central to a lot of the walks you will find in this book. Yet Shropshire is often ignored as a 'hill walking' county by regular outdoor enthusiasts, which is surprising when you consider how extensive the upland regions of the county are.

But although a lot of visitors to Shropshire think only of the Long Mynd when they assess the walking potential available to them, there is so very much more to be had and the purpose of this small volume is to show you where it is and how to explore it. Beyond the mass of The Long Mynd you will find the exciting line of narrow hills that border the east of the A49 – The Lawley, Caer Caradoc, Ragleth Hill and The Hope Bowdler Range with the delightful escarpment of Wenlock Edge beyond them again. And there is also the ever popular (and always lovely) 'Wrekin', providing an outlying top further to the east.

On the west of the Long Mynd you will find the legendary Stiperstones, which provide one of Shropshire's best ridge walks and some of its roughest walking. Not too far away from this are The Betchcott Hills.

Also I must mention The Clee Hills. These are more southerly than the other tops. Brown Clee Hill is Shropshire's highest point at 1,772ft (533 metres) and makes a superb outing at anytime of the year.

These are friendly hills where you can walk for hour upon contented hour on fine days. However, please do take the usual precautions when venturing into hill country anywhere – let someone know where you are going and when you will be back, and get an up to date forecast for the weather. Appropriate clothing should always be worn and a good pair of boots are essential, and will make some of the rougher ground easier to walk over.

All of these routes are on rights of way or over open access land, and the Cardingmill Valley and Church Stretton have excellent visitor and information centres.

Enjoy your walking!

THE LAWLEY

DESCRIPTION This is arguably one of the best ridge walks to be found in Shropshire's varied hill country. At 1,236ft (377 metres) it's a respectable height and the narrow crest of the ridge runs for almost two miles. Views are superb in all directions. This route of 3½ miles does a complete circuit of this wonderful summit and starts by following the lovely ridge over the rocky top and then down the steep south west flank, with a return being accomplished via the atmospheric and lonely track (footpath/bridleway) along the north west base of the hill. Allow 2½ hours.

START From the Lawley car park on a minor lane at the northern end of The Lawley (slightly north east of Leebotwood). SO 505990.

DIRECTIONS From Leebotwood on the A49 either take the minor road in the village centre west going LEFT at the next T-junction and then RIGHT at the next crossroads to reach the car park, or go west off the A49 a little north of Leebotwood near Longnor, keeping RIGHT at the next junction and ahead at the crossroads to reach the same point. Whichever way you use be aware these are narrow roads and need extra care when driving on them. The car park is free and will take four or five cars if parked carefully.

1 Exit the car park at the rear following the footpath to rise up steeply on a good path through woodland and next to a fence. Reach a gate, pass through and enter access land. Climb up through the trees on the path at the start of the Lawley ridge. As the trees begin to thin follow the distinct path onto the open fellside and head up the ridge. The path is never in doubt and rises up, gently at first, towards the distant pole visible on the summit. Climb over a few minor bumps and arrive below the summit cone, where a very steep pull on a decent path brings you to the high marker pole on the rocky top.

2 From the summit continue along the ridge in a south-westerly direction following the good path and descending

gradually towards the bulk of Caer Caradoc ahead. After a while the ridge begins to drop more steeply towards the valley floor and finally plunges down to curve slightly RIGHT near the bottom to reach a gate near to buildings.

3 Pass through the gate and carry on straight ahead going to the right of the buildings on a grassy path to reach a cart track. Here go RIGHT following this track until it goes sharp left and, when it does go straight ahead, towards a gate and a sign for 'The Lawley'. Pass through the gate and continue along the good bridleway on the west side of the hill. The excellent track climbs gradually for a while before descending through trees to reach open ground again and eventually reaching a large cream house on the left.

4 Continue ahead on the widening track to reach a cattle grid and gate. Continue on the other side eventually descending to pass a red roofed house on the right-hand side and reach a lane at a signpost. Here go RIGHT steeply up the lane and back to the car park.

*T*he Lawley, *at 1,236ft above sea level, is not one of the highest of Shropshire's hills but it is easily recognised and attractive. Running alongside the busy A49 as it does, with the distinctive pole on the summit (common on Shropshire hills) that sports a weather vane, many walkers pass it each year on their way to climb the more famous Caer Caradoc which is its near neighbour. In missing The Lawley out they are by-passing one of the best of all Shropshire Hill walks.*

The two mile ridge alone makes the effort required to climb this top more than worthwhile and the rocky summit area is a great vantage point, providing a top that many a higher mountain would be very proud of. There are the remains of an Iron Age hill fort on the uppermost reaches and it would have been a superb and easily defended location for such a structure, but very little of it now remains and it takes a skilled eye to pick out the dyke that runs across the summit to the south.

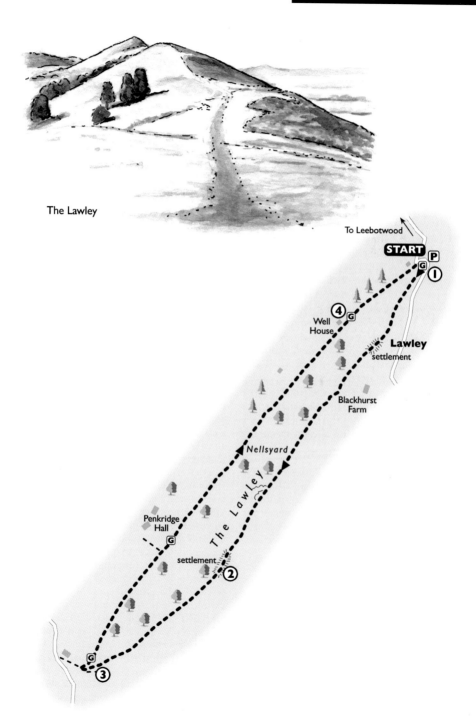

The Lawley

To Leebotwood

START

P

G

I

4 G

Well
House

Lawley
settlement

Blackhurst
Farm

Nellsyard

The Lawley

Penkridge
Hall

G

settlement

2

G

3

A CAER CARADOC CIRCUIT

DESCRIPTION Caer Caradoc is a magnet. It is a popular outing done in either an up-and-down-the-same-way trip or by combining several of the footpaths and tracks to give a decent circular walk. Great views, a really high level hill walking outing and plenty of ups and downs all combine to give this 5¾ mile route a very distinctive flavour. It's a great way to get the feeling for this particular area of the Shropshire hills. Allow 4 hours to do it comfortably.

START From The Co-operative supermarket shoppers and 'Walkers Welcome' car park in the centre of Church Stretton. This is pay and display, and there are toilets. SO 454936.

DIRECTIONS From the traffic lights on the A49 at Church Stretton go either LEFT if coming from the south or RIGHT if coming from the north to drive up the main street over the railway bridge and turn LEFT, once past the antique market, into Easthope Road. A little further along here you pass the toilets on the right and you then go RIGHT in front of the supermarket to turn RIGHT into the car park.

I Exit the car park going LEFT along the road to pass the toilets and the antique market and then go RIGHT at the T junction to head down the main road, staying on the right to cross the railway bridge and reach the traffic lights on the A49. Use the lights to cross the road continuing ahead signposted 'Sandford Avenue'. A little way up this road cross over by a white chapel to turn LEFT down Watling Street North and carry on along this until the road bends right. At this point go LEFT signposted 'Caer Caradoc' and follow this minor lane until it ends near the buildings of Eastwood, which are on the right. Here go RIGHT over a stile by a gate and enter a large field. Follow the RIGHT-hand edge of the field and curve gently LEFT with a stream below right. When the fence (right) ends near a gate continue ahead to pick up a track by fence posts. Follow this to curve RIGHT into the field corner and here reach a gate, with ponds on the left.

2 Pass through the gate to continue along a good green lane with a brook down left. Take a path forking LEFT a little way along it to descend to a bridge over the brook, and go RIGHT ignoring a left turning uphill. Start climbing up the valley with a stream right and continue to re-join a good track a little further on and going LEFT. This track rises up the lower East slopes of Caer Caradoc climbing steadily to reach a gate. Pass through and continue on the track now ignoring any footpaths going left or right. Pass the ruins of Cwms Cottage (right) and continue to reach two public footpath signs near a stile on the left.

3 Cross the stile to head half RIGHT on trackless ground going to the right of Robins Tump and towards the Lawley ahead. Pass through a gate and in a short distance cross a stile on the right to go down the left side of the next field leaving the edge after a while to make a way down the middle of this narrow field heading into trees ahead. There is little path at this point but continue to drop to a bridge over a brook, cross this and continue through woods on a path to reach a stile. Cross this, walking towards a house ahead Go LEFT on a cart track just before the house and after a public footpath sign. Climb steeply to go to the left of an old house and curve RIGHT to go around it towards a marker post. Follow the path heading slightly LEFT of the Lawley, crossing heath land and staying LEFT when the path splits to head towards a fence to the LEFT. Reach a stile in the fence and cross to go onto the access lane of Little Caradoc. Leave the footpath to head steeply uphill on trackless ground going to the LEFT of a tree and keep climbing to pick up a grass path near a hollow on the right. Go LEFT on the path for a while, leaving it shortly to go RIGHT past a prominent boulder and then climb to join a good path going LEFT. Turn off it to the RIGHT to go to the highest point of Little Caradoc and return back to path to follow it RIGHT to descend to a col with a stile by a pile of stones.

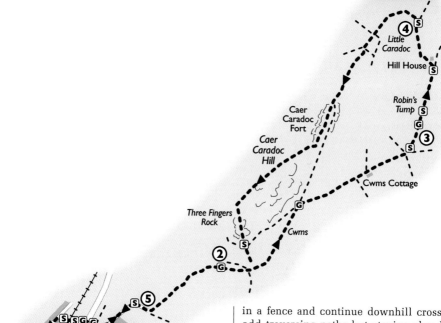

Three Fingers Rock

Cwms

Caer Caradoc Hill

Caer Caradoc Fort

Cwms Cottage

Little Caradoc

Hill House

Robin's Tump

Church Stretton

START

in a fence and continue downhill crossing odd traversing paths but staying ahead to finally reach a T-junction near a ford. Here go RIGHT on your outbound route crossing a bridge, going RIGHT and continuing back to a gate. Pass through and follow the field edge back to a stile.

4 Cross the stile and go up the right side of the fence and climb to pick up the good path climbing the north ridge of Caer Caradoc, crossing a cart track near a gate and keeping ahead when the fence ends. Climb up the good path curving LEFT near the top and then RIGHT to pass through the ramparts of the old hill fort to reach the summit area. From here head down keeping to the right of the summit plateau heading towards Church Stretton far below. Curve RIGHT as the path descends and, as the path gets a bit fainter and after some outcrops on the left, turn sharply RIGHT to pass through the fort ramparts again continuing to pass large gully (right). Descend towards Three Fingers Rock following a good path along the ridge. After a few ups and downs join a fence (left) reaching Three Fingers Rock and leaving the path to go to the RIGHT of it curving LEFT in front of it to drop to join a path and go LEFT back onto a good path to continue to descend the ridge. Cross a stile

5 Cross and go LEFT down the lane. At the junction go RIGHT for a few metres and then go RIGHT through gate by a small building. Walk down the field to reach the A49 via a kissing gate. Cross carefully to go though a kissing gate on the other side and enter a field by playing fields. Go straight on along the field edge to cross a stile in the field corner and descend to a railway line. Cross this carefully to cross another stile on the other side and follow footpath to the right of buildings (Windsor Place) and rise up to join the lane going LEFT along it. Stay LEFT at the junction and walk back to join the main road near the Police Station. Walk RIGHT along the road to cross over shortly and go LEFT back up Easthope Road to walk back to carpark.

C *aer Caradoc was once the home of the Cornovii, and was also at one time stronghold of the ancient Briton Caractacus.*

5

SHROPSHIRE'S THREE PEAKS

DESCRIPTION The double summit of Hope Bowdler Hill feels like two distinct and separate tops and there can be no doubting the claim of Willstone Hill to be treated individually. There are great views throughout and the route climbs from the lovely town of Church Stretton to curve below mighty Caer Caradoc using delightful forest and hill paths and tracks to gain a high ridge at a col between Willstone Hill and Hope Bowdler Hill. An 'out and back' trip to Willstone Hill is followed by one of Shropshire's best ridge walks descending back to the fields again and returning to the start via a combination of interestingly linked field paths. The ridge alone makes this 5¼ mile walk worth the effort, but the whole route is a great day out and can easily be done in 3 hours.

START From the Co-operative supermarket shoppers and 'Walkers Welcome' car park in the centre of Church Stretton. This is pay and display, and there are toilets. SO 454936.

DIRECTIONS From the traffic lights on the A49 at Church Stretton go either LEFT if coming from the south or RIGHT if coming from the north to drive up the main street over the railway bridge and turn LEFT once past the antique market into Easthope Road. A little along here you pass the toilets on the right and you then go RIGHT in front of the supermarket to go RIGHT into the car park.

I Exit the car park going LEFT along the road to pass the toilets and the antique market and then go RIGHT at the T junction to head down the main road, staying on the right to cross the railway bridge and reach the traffic lights on the A49. Use the lights to cross the road continuing ahead signposted 'Sandford Avenue'. A little way up this road cross over by a white chapel to turn LEFT down Watling Street North and carry on along this until the road bends right. At this point go LEFT signposted 'Caer Caradoc'

and follow this minor lane until it ends near the buildings of 'Eastwood', which are on the right. Here go RIGHT over a stile by a gate to enter a large field. Follow the right-hand edge of the field and curve gently LEFT with a stream below RIGHT. When the fence (right) ends near a gate, continue ahead to pick up a track by fence posts. Follow this to curve RIGHT into the field corner and here reach a gate with ponds right. Pass through and continue on the track, staying ahead when the track forks left down to a brook. Just before a ford go RIGHT up a track by fence on the right to reach a gate.

2 Pass though the gate, climbing on a good path through trees with a fence on the right. As the trees end, curve LEFT and RIGHT following the path to cross a stile by a gate. Rise up the next field (trackless) joining a track and going LEFT to pass through a gate (usually open) and follow the marker arrow to go RIGHT behind 'Cwms Farm' and leave the main track. Pass through a gate in the fence (right) to go LEFT on the traversing path and climb steadily to descend a bit and stay LEFT when the path splits. Reach a T junction near a fence/finger post and go RIGHT uphill climbing to a col. Cross the stile on the left near a fence corner and continue with the fence on your right, passing through a gate opening near a stile and heading LEFT to the summit of Willstone Hill. From the summit, Re-trace your steps to re-join your outbound route at the wall corner crossing the stile to the col.

3 Cross the track heading south west and climbing on the good path to the summit of Hope Bowdler Hill. Continue in the same direction to descend to a col with a sheepfold and climb south west again to reach the second summit, where there is a cairn. Follow the descending ridge in a south westerly direction to pass a large outcrop and continuing to reach a stile in a fence. Go RIGHT descending to pass through a gate and follow the left of the field (trackless) passing through a gate in the bottom left corner of the field. Go LEFT along the track to reach a road.

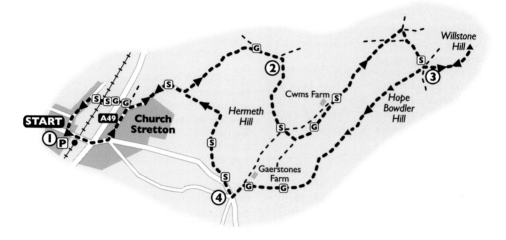

4 Go RIGHT along the road (taking care) to go RIGHT as the road bends left at a footpath sign. Rise to cross a stile and follow the footpath along the left-hand side of the next field to cross a stile in the left field corner, going RIGHT up the right-hand side of the next field reaching a stile in the right-hand field corner. Ignore this and go LEFT down the field (trackless) keeping on the right to go LEFT, then RIGHT, of the house to cross a stile in the field corner.

5 Go LEFT to walk to a junction on your outbound route and go RIGHT, going RIGHT again in a short while through a gate near a small building, to walk over a field passing through a kissing gate to reach the busy A49. Cross carefully going through a kissing gate near a play area (left) and continue down the left-hand side of the field crossing a railway (carefully) via two stiles. Once over, go to the RIGHT of the rest home following the footpath sign to walk up the right-hand side of it. At the road, go LEFT to stay LEFT at the road end and curve RIGHT to enter Church Stretton after the Police Station. Cross over the road go RIGHT for a short way, then to go LEFT to walk back to the car park

Hope Bowdler will be seen to the south east of the ridge. The manor house here was once the home of Edric Sauvage, who was also known by the colourful name of 'Wild Eric'. He was a Saxon who continued to fight after the Norman conquest of England and became notorious as a rebel and scourge of patrolling Norman troops.

RAGLETH HILL

DESCRIPTION Ragleth Hill is the quietest of the trio of similar summits that border the east side of the A49. It is the most southerly and the ground beyond it drops dramatically away, making its top a fine viewpoint. This route climbs from a minor road through farmland and steeply up the northern end of the ridge. It then meanders along it with awesome views down both sides. From the summit, a steep descent drops back to the fields of rural Shropshire. 4¼ miles. Allow 3 hours.

START There is space to park cars on the edge of the minor road that runs through Ragdon, along the south east side of Ragleth Hill. If you are driving south west (the best approach) down this minor lane parking is just after the junction (left) for Chelmick and Soudley. Please park considerately and don't block drives or gates. SO 460922.

DIRECTIONS At Church Stretton go either right if coming from the south or left if coming from the north to drive beyond the houses and continuing for about half a mile from the lights. Just before a car parking area on the left you will find two lanes leaving the main road on the right. Take the second of these to reach the parking area for this route.

1 Walk north east along the road past the junction to pass Ragdon cottage (left) and take a footpath LEFT a little further on at Dryhill Farm, following the access track and passing through a gate near a stile. Go ahead when the access track bears left climbing a grassy path to a stile and gate. Cross this, continuing over the field to cross another stile by a gate. Leave the fence and climb half LEFT staying RIGHT and following the arrow at a path split and curving LEFT at a finger post to the ridge end.

2 Take the good ridge path south-west, rising on a good track amidst the fern and eventually descending to a col before climbing again to the summit of Ragleth Hill and the high pole.

3 Continue south west, dropping steeply on a fainter path to go LEFT at an outcrop, then RIGHT at a fingerpost near a fence and cross a stile. Go RIGHT following the path to the right of a plantation and pass a marker post, going RIGHT at a larger post and taking the track descending into a wooded valley to pass through two gates near a bench. Continue to a stile and continuing to the RIGHT of a house and walk to a lane. Go LEFT passing through a gate to go LEFT of a house and RIGHT of a barn to pass through a gate (footpath sign) and rise on a path through woods. Cross a stile on the RIGHT just before a gate, following the path and going RIGHT of the fence corner to descend next to a fence on your left to a bridge.

4 Cross the bridge, rising up to cross a stile, and go up the left side of the field. Reach a stile but don't go over, instead turn RIGHT along the left edge of the field to pass through a gate, going LEFT through another gate in a hedge in a short distance. Walk down the right of this field to reach a track via a gate. Descend to pass through a gate opening and continue to a junction. Go LEFT before the next gate to go LEFT of the pond on a good track, continuing to gates. Go through the gate, following with the footpath markers to take the footpath along the left of the field. Pass through a gate curving around the left of the next field to reach a stile. Don't cross but go RIGHT towards the brook and hollow crossing a stile by a gate and taking the track beyond, curving RIGHT and LEFT and rising to exit to a lane via a gate.

5 Cross the lane to go RIGHT of a bench, entering the field ahead via a gate. Go down the right-hand side of the field to pass through a gate in a field corner to the left of a kissing gate. Cross two more fields and stiles going LEFT after the second one to cross another stile in a field corner and go half RIGHT to cross a stile going half RIGHT to follow a hedge to cross a stile. Go to the RIGHT of the bungalow, crossing a stile and continuing over a track and through a gate opening and through the farmyard exiting via a stile and continuing along the right-hand side of the next field. Cross a stile

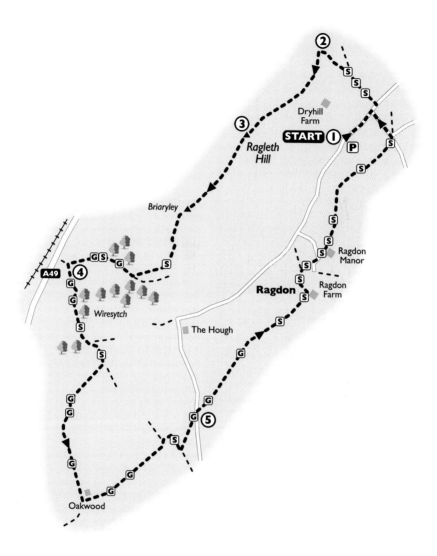

going along the left of the next field (near the fence) to descend into a meadow curving RIGHT and climbing to cross a stile. Climb over the field to a fence corner continuing ahead on the left-hand side of the fence to drop to exit to a lane via a stile. Go LEFT to go LEFT at the junction to return to your car.

WALK 5

THE WREKIN

DESCRIPTION This delightful little summit is one of the most easterly of these routes in Shropshire's hill country, and because of its elevated and isolated position, the views in all directions, especially to the Church Stretton Hills and Wenlock Edge, are magnificent. This route climbs through woodland to follow the ridge to the summit and then continues, staying on the ridge, to traverse the hill to the other end returning through the woodland that covers the lower flanks of this lovely top. Care is needed to keep on the right path in the woods on the return journey. This can also be muddy after rain. At just under 4¼ miles, this circuit should take between 2½ and 3 hours .

START From The Wrekin and Ercall car park (free) in a large quarry close to the westerly end of the M54 motorway. This is a popular destination and you will need to arrive early at weekends to get a place – or visit later in the afternoon. SJ 638092.

DIRECTIONS Access to the car park for The Wrekin is made easy by using the M54. You need junction 7, which is the last junction at the western end of the motorway. Once off the M54 follow the minor road south east towards Little Wenlock to a junction on a bend with another minor lane. Go straight on towards Little Wenlock and the car park is located on the left.

1 Leave the car park with the quarry to the right, exiting onto a lane to go RIGHT and then LEFT at the road junction as the lane bends right. Continue ahead for a short distance to go back LEFT, passing through a gateway and going up the track to pass by old toilets. Climb steadily through the trees on the good wide path and at the first major path junction, turn back RIGHT to climb steeply up a good track. Continue to reach leveller ground and pass a café to reach gates and a stile/gap in a fence.

2 Pass through the gap going LEFT up The Wrekin ridge in a south westerly direction, to go LEFT at a path junction reached and climb up the ridge using the good path to exit the trees onto the narrowing ridge. Follow the ridge, with good views right and left, until it curves left near a hill fort sign to climb again, then levels off near a plantation on the right, and finally rises up again. Stay ahead when a path junction is reached on level ground to pass through the old fort earthworks. Pass the mast on the left hand side to continue to the trig point and viewfinder on the summit. *Take time to explore the vicinity here as there are some great views to be had by walking to the edges directly close to the trig point.*

3 Follow the path south-west from the summit, descending to pass through the fort earthworks again, and passing rocks on their right side. Descend on the ridge into trees again, continuing to follow the ridge down on steeper ground to finally reach a cart track as the terrain becomes flatter. Cross over to rise up beyond it to the wooded top of Little Hill. Go half LEFT following the narrow path down through the trees. As the path levels, continue to cross two more tracks. Follow a sunken path through the woods keeping ahead at a path crossroads to curve slightly RIGHT to pass to the left of a gate and reach a lane.

4 Go LEFT down this lane and in a short distance, at a parking area on the left, go LEFT to go right of a barrier, heading north-east into the woods again and curving RIGHT with the path into the trees. Rise with the path and stay ahead when the track curves left up hill. Continue rising to reach a permissive path at a T junction of tracks.

5 Go RIGHT here still climbing through the trees to reach a path junction near a gate and go LEFT to climb up again on a track, still in the trees. Stay ahead at a path junction on the left and eventually reach level ground for a short while and then begin to drop down. Climb up and down for a while and after a gate down to the right, reach a path junction and go ahead, descending to join your outbound route back to the lane to go RIGHT and walk back to the car park.

10

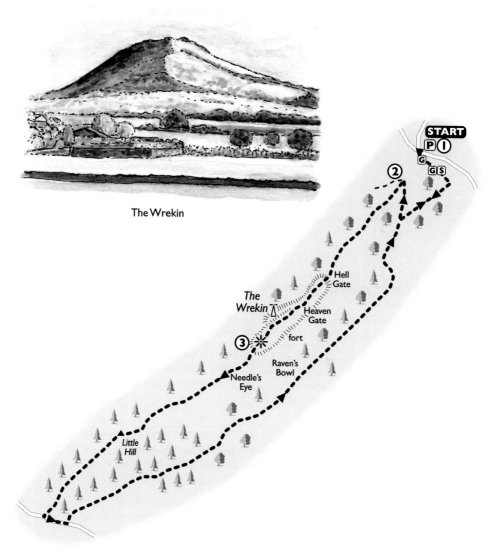

The Wrekin

The top of **The Wrekin** seems much higher than its 1,335ft (407 metres). Local legend has it that you can see fifteen counties from this point if the visibility is good. The hill fort on the summit is Iron Age and covers about eight hectares. It was thought to have been built by the Cornovii Tribe and used as their capital. Tolkien is said to have used The Wrekin as the inspiration for Middle Earth in his 'Lord of The Rings' trilogy, as he lived nearby during his lifetime. Legends abound here and the most popular concerns a Welsh giant who 'created' The Wrekin by taking a spade full of earth to dump in the River Severn to flood nearby Shrewsbury. Tiring of his journey and getting fed up with the idea, he dumped his earth in a great pile near Wellington, and The Wrekin was formed.

A WENLOCK EDGE CIRCUIT

DESCRIPTION Wenlock Edge is the narrow wedge of elevated land that runs for almost fifteen miles from Craven Arms to Much Wenlock. The wooded limestone hillside drops steeply to the north west and the flatter lands of the north Shropshire plain. This section takes in Blakeway Hollow and the superb viewpoint of Majors Leap. This route starts high up and just below the edge, and climbs up to follow the atmospheric Blakeway Hollow continuing to join Wenlock Edge and following it along the crest above the trees of Blakeway Coppice. You can finish off with a trip into nearby Much Wenlock or by a short 15 minute drive to take in Thomas Telford's awe inspiring Iron Bridge at the aptly named town of Iron Bridge. 3¾ miles long, it will take you about 2½ hours.

START There is a free National Trust car park on the B4371 about half a mile west of Much Wenlock, on the right side of the road under Wenlock Edge. SO 612996.

DIRECTIONS From Much Wenlock go west on the B4371 Church Stretton road for about ½ mile, where you will find it on the right.

I Leave the carpark past the information board taking the rising track in trees to pass through a rock gap to a very rough track (Blakeway Hollow) and go LEFT to walk along it. The track rises gently between high banks and wooded edges. Follow the hollow and continue to rise for half a mile or so and eventually reach a large path junction amongst trees, with a National Trust sign for 'Wenlock Edge' and a footpath sign for Blakeway Coppice and Harley Bank.

2 Go LEFT towards a gate but go LEFT again almost immediately to take a footpath and pass by a wooden barrier. This is signposted 'Majors Leap Walk'. Walk along the woodland edge with a fence left and open country beyond. This section can be very muddy after rain. Follow the edge of the woods rising up slightly. Continue along

the crest of Wenlock Edge with a big quarry opening up to your left. *There are occasional views through the trees to the right off 'The Edge' and down to the Shropshire Plain below. This is true A. E. Houseman country. Author of the classic 'A Shropshire Lad', Houseman was a Shropshire man through and through and the escarpment and rolling terrain of the fifteen mile long Wenlock Edge is very typical of the county he loved so much.* Continue on as the quarry vanishes behind trees and look for a turning on the right signposted 'Majors Leap'. Take this and climb to the viewpoint returning the same way to the edge track, and going RIGHT along it. Continue through the woodland with a fence still left. Enter more open ground and carry on to enter trees again. Pass (and visit) a viewpoint for 'The Wrekin' on the right and then continue on the good path to eventually reach more open ground with the main part of the large quarry now below left. There are good views of Brown Clee Hill (Shropshire's highest point) also over to the left. Continue to a path junction with a finger post showing 'Majors Leap Walk' going right.

3 Go RIGHT following 'Majors Leap Walk' and leave the crest of 'The Edge' descending steeply to pass a gate on the left side. Continue to descend steeply taking care if the ground is wet. Continue to go RIGHT on another track when your reach it, now deep in the forest itself, with 'The Edge' above you right. You are still on 'Majors Leap Walk'. Curve RIGHT and start to climb up again and reach a path junction.

4 Take the RIGHT fork signposted for 'Much Wenlock' and continue on this path rising gradually through the trees. Continue past steps going up right signposted 'Majors Leap' and continue up through the woods. After a footpath leaves to the left begin to climb more steeply through the trees and climb back to pass by a gate on the right-hand side to arrive back at the major path junction from your outbound route. Go LEFT signposted 'Harley Bank' and descend through the trees staying RIGHT as the path splits a little further on (the left fork heading down a narrow hollow)

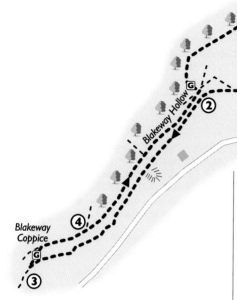

and continue in the same direction to pass a finger post and right turning further on. Carry on descending steeply through the woods and then fork RIGHT on an uphill track signposted 'Jenny Wind Walk'. A little further on fork RIGHT again (by a post with 'Harley Bank', 'Jenny Wind Walk' and Much Wenlock' on it) and climb up through the trees to curve LEFT as the angle eases and follow the path to pass a small fence and

reach a mile stone marker, a path/track junction and a gate on the right.

5 Go RIGHT through two gates and walk towards Stokes Barns ahead. Reach a gate by a stile and pass through and then through another one. Walk down a track between two fences to go through a kissing gate on the right signposted 'National Trust car park'. Cross the access drive going left of the buildings and take the path ahead over the grass towards a gate and signpost. Go RIGHT of the gate (signposted 'National Trust car park') and follow a narrow path to pass through another gate following the path beyond between hedges and then descend more steeply following the path as best you can. Reach a path junction at a footpath for Harley Bank and go LEFT, then go RIGHT down steps to go through two gates and across the grass back to the car park.

THE ASCENT OF BROWN CLEE HILL

SHROPSHIRE'S HIGHEST POINT

DESCRIPTION At 1,772 feet, this is the county's highest point, and also a wonderful walk with great views and some rugged moorland to boot. When you reach the view finder on the summit, the panorama towards the Long Mynd and Titterstone Clee Hill and the whole of Shropshire seems to be laid out below you. A return is made through the plantations of Big Wood and good use of forest trails and tracks is made. This route is 5¼ miles long and will take you about 3½ hours.

START There is space to park cars on the edge of the minor road that runs close to the eastern side of Brown Clee Hill. Here you will find the start of a forest trail and a somewhat overgrown picnic area. From Cleobury North take the minor road towards Ditton Priors and take the first left turning you come to. Follow this lane and when it bends sharp right continue a short way to find the parking area on the right. SO 607873.

DIRECTIONS Take the A49 to Ludlow, and then take the A4117 leaving it to follow the B4364 to Cleobury North (best if coming from southerly directions) or if coming from the north aim to get to Bridgnorth (west of Wolverhampton) perhaps using the A442 and from here pick up the B4364 again.

I Walk up the lane in a north-westerly direction to the end of the parking area and take a footpath through a gate on the LEFT next to a stile and another gate. Follow the good path beyond curving immediately RIGHT following the sign for 'Forest Trail'. Rise gently on the path and gradually curve back LEFT continuing to climb up the hillside, passing a bench and continuing to enter woodland passing another bench. The track becomes wider and enters the forest proper. Stay LEFT when it splits, rising to go

LEFT on a forest track at a T-junction. Walk into a more open forest area and shortly go RIGHT to pass through a gate (yellow arrow) by a big gate. Continue uphill on the track through trees, climbing steadily as the trees clear a little and then get thicker again. Continue to pass through a gate and cross a track following the path beyond through trees to join a track coming in from the left. Go RIGHT on this continuing uphill. Continue to climb up a steep bank and exit the trees. Climb through a meadow with an old wall and old buildings on the right. Walk ahead and a little LEFT when the path splits to climb steadily up to the head of the meadow, and once over a steep bank you reach more level ground and come to a road.

2 Go LEFT along the road to cross a stile or go through a gate to the left of a cattle grid and continue on the road. Just before the road curves right towards the relay station gates, go LEFT at a fingerpost to climb to the view finder and summit of Brown Clee Hill. *Many people claim it is possible to see fourteen counties from here on a clear day. Coal, stone and iron have all been mined on this summit.*

3 Drop back down the steps going RIGHT when the steps go left. Descend a good path over the moor heading for a fence to reach a finger post just before the fence with a gate ahead. Here go LEFT on the Shropshire Way taking the path to the left of the fence. Stay on the left of the fence to begin a gradual descent. When the fence cuts sharp right continue ahead descending the path towards trees below. Go straight over a crossroad of paths heading for a wide col to reach a bench on the left and pass through a gate in a fence to reach the col above the area known as 'Five Springs'.

4 Cross straight over the col, following The Shropshire Way to pick up a fainter path heading uphill. There are several options to take at this point but the best one to go with is the one that stays close to the wall/fence and trees left. When these trees end continue uphill by the wall to reach more trees left. As the summit gets near, curve RIGHT to reach a better track and climb to the summit of Clee Burf, reaching a gate to the left of the relay station. Cross the stile and walk to the rocks on the unmarked highest point.

5 Re-trace your steps back to the broad col to go RIGHT to pass through a gate in the fence near a finger post. Follow a yellow arrow into the trees to pass through an opening to the right of a gate and the left of a fence end. Stay on the good track going to the LEFT of a small fence ahead. Pick up a track going to the RIGHT of a finger post and follow the yellow arrow to head towards more trees. Pass through a gate opening to descend to a gate. Pass through to continue on the track descending to join another track at a finger post and going LEFT along it. This curves gradually left to pass through another gate opening and stays LEFT when the track splits going LEFT of a house. Rise slightly on the track continuing ahead at a finger post and staying on the track. Descend to join a road and then leave it immediately, going ahead to pick up a track again going into the trees. Shortly re-join your outbound route at gates (left) to continue ahead going half RIGHT just before two gates. Follow your outbound route downhill ignoring the first turning on the right but going RIGHT at a bench (left) with a post ahead. Descend to pass through an unusual gate in the fence and follow the path downhill through the picnic area to pass through a gate to the lane and the parking area.

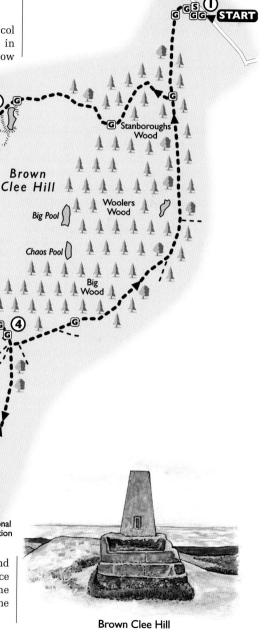

Brown Clee Hill

WALK 8

SHORT BUT SWEET

AN ASCENT OF TITTERSTONE CLEE HILL

DESCRIPTION The satellite station on the 1,748ft (533 metres) summit of Titterstone Clee Hill is a prominent sight from many places. This has a reputation of being a 'spoilt summit', with major quarry-working-remains all over it and a road almost to the top. However the quarry workings are long abandoned and overgrown and what remains provides a fascinating insight to the mineral wealth of this region and the way man sought to win it. *Do take care around the old workings as many are unsafe.* This walk climbs steep and airy slopes, visits a superb viewpoint and walks along an exposed edge with dramatic views dropping away on both sides. *Avoid this walk in bad weather.* This walk is approximately 1 mile and takes about 30 minutes.

START There is a large car park (SO 593775) amongst the old quarry workings at the end of the public road leading up towards the satellite station, where you can park free of charge. You will find the road leaving the A4117 about a mile west of the village of Cleehill – it is signposted for the top.

DIRECTIONS You will find the A4117 signposted off the Ludlow by-pass, with the summit of Titterstone Clee Hill prominent to confirm the direction. From Bridgnorth the B4364 will take you to the A4117 and it can also be picked up off the A456 west of Kidderminster.

I Leave the car park, heading towards the old quarry area and in the direction of the summit of Titterstone Clee Hill. Go to the LEFT of a mound following the path towards eroded and steep paths on the hillside ahead. Walk through the old quarry towards the steep, grassy spoil heaps ahead. Continue towards the slopes and just before you reach them turn LEFT on a good track. As the track bends left in a short distance, leave it going RIGHT past a small boulder to take a path going half LEFT and cutting across the steep face of the hill. Turn back RIGHT following the path (faint at first) to follow the quarry edge (it will be on your right) and rise steeply up. After a while curve LEFT away from the edge to zigzag slightly, still climbing. Turn RIGHT as a better path is reached climbing up a grassy groove to reach the head of a gully (right). Here turn half LEFT over a short trackless section to pick up a path and go half LEFT on it, and then stay RIGHT when it splits to head towards a line of fence posts climbing up the hillside. Just before the second fence post turn LEFT taking a path uphill and climbing up to the summit of Titterstone Clee Hill, reaching the trig and the wind shelter.

2 From the summit trig turn to face the satellite station and take a path half LEFT following it around the summit edge and leaving it shortly to walk slightly LEFT to the prominent rock outcrop and viewpoint of 'Giants Chair'.

3 Re-trace your steps back to the trig but don't go to it. Instead go LEFT on a path that goes to the RIGHT of the satellite station. Ignore the road left at the entrance to the station and stay on the path following a line of fence posts with a large quarry below left and the car park down right. Continue downhill in the same direction to veer back RIGHT on the now good track and descend to join a road.

4 Go RIGHT along this road to walk the short distance back to the car park.

The Clee Hills (both Titterstone Clee and Brown Clee – Shropshire's highest) bear the scars of our predecessors' relentless struggle to extract the mineral wealth they contain in great abundance. Various forms of stone, iron and coal have been mined for here and as this was done in an age where conservation meant less than general survival, the results of this activity have been left lying around in the form of abandoned mine workings, buildings and spoil heaps.

Titterstone Clee
(50 years ago)

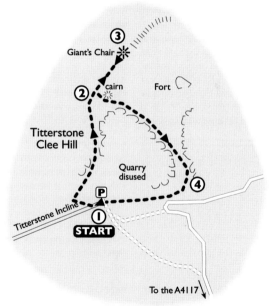

However, the picture is not as bleak as it would seem as much of the damage is now 'naturalising' and there is a haunting beauty in overgrown buildings, and even spoil heaps have a certain something about them as nature covers their nakedness. The satellite station on the summit is a civil aviation tracking one, and is much larger once reached than it appears from below. There are also the indistinct remains of an Iron Age hill fort on the top.

HOPESAY HILL

DESCRIPTION Hopesay Hill is often overlooked by walkers in Shropshire, and this is a great shame. It is a shy and retiring little summit of just over 1,033ft in height and makes a great destination for a quiet morning or afternoon stroll amidst rolling hill country. The route described here is 2½ miles long and will take about two hours to complete at a leisurely pace. The route starts at the pretty hamlet of Hopesay, surrounded by hill country, and after climbing steeply to the ridge line a high level walk follows before the route then drops back to the valley and returns to Hopesay via a quiet lane. The descent from the ridge to the fields below can be difficult to follow in summer as the fern grows very high here and the path tends to get lost in it. Come here in spring, autumn or winter and give the warmer months a miss.

START There is space to park cars on the roadside in Hopesay Village but please be considerate and don't block drives or access points. This is a small village and is lovely and quiet – please keep it that way. Hopesay is best reached from Craven Arms on the A49 and is accessed via winding narrow lanes where care is required. ST 390333.

DIRECTIONS Hopesay is slightly north west of Craven Arms on the B4368, then take the minor road north to Hopesay from Aston on Clun.

I Walk up the lane heading out of Hopesay Village in a southerly direction following The Shropshire Way and passing a post box and phone box. Pass a bench on the left and walk out of the village after the house of 'Fairhead'. Continue on the lane passing an access drive and reaching a public footpath sign on the left. Go LEFT through the kissing gate to follow the left-hand side of a field, crossing a bridge over a brook and going straight over the next field. Cross a stile in the fence and climb directly up the next field on a good path heading for the trees above. Climb to pass through a kissing gate in a field corner, walking forward a few paces and staying LEFT when the path splits. Go LEFT through a gate to enter open access land. Walk ahead for a few paces to go RIGHT up a good path climbing Hopesay Hill. Rise between ferns to pass a finger post near bushes and continue. Head to the RIGHT of trees ahead passing them on the right-hand side and staying with the path as the angle eases and you reach the unmarked lower summit of Hopesay Hill.

2 Continue in the same direction descending to a marshy depression and heading for the fence ahead. Once the fence is reached at a stile/gate and signpost go LEFT, staying to the left of the fence and following the path that rises up the main summit area of Hopesay Hill. Climb over the brow of the hill and continue on down the other side keeping the fence to the right. Pass a stile and continue ahead to reach a fence corner with a gate and a stile on the right.

3 Go half LEFT from the stile following the direction of the arrow walking towards Burrow Hill ahead. There is a very faint path and it is not easy to follow, but it develops as you descend slightly. If unsure of the direction descend towards the last large tree ahead and you should find the path getting better. Now follow the path down through the fern to reach a stile in the fence line below (not visible when heather is high). If it is summer and the heather is very high you can either aim to follow the path as best you can – though it is very difficult – you usually end up hitting the fence too far to the left and having to follow it back right to the stile. If you have a GPS unit with you enter the co-ordinates ST39048/33396 and this will bring you to the stile.

4 Once the stile is reached cross it and very shortly go over another to enter a field and walk down the right-hand side of it to cross a stile in the right-hand corner of the field. Descend on the right-hand edge of the next field to cross a stile in the right corner and enter the grounds of a house. Curve LEFT to pick up the access drive going RIGHT to walk down it to pass through a gate and reach a lane.

Hopesay Common

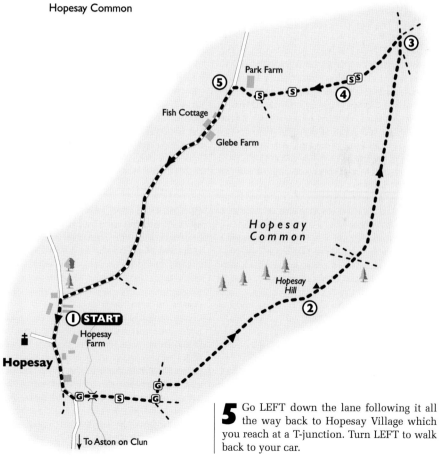

5 Go LEFT down the lane following it all the way back to Hopesay Village which you reach at a T-junction. Turn LEFT to walk back to your car.

THE STIPERSTONES RIDGE

DESCRIPTION The unmistakable rugged outline of the Stiperstones Ridge is one of Shropshire's well known hill landmarks. The north end is the most dramatic and care is needed here. 6 miles long, allow 4½ hours.

START Use the main Stiperstones car parking area (free). This is located east of the A488 and between the hamlets of The Bog and Kinnerton, high on minor roads. SO 369977.

DIRECTIONS The Stiperstones are close to the A488 and near the hamlet of Stiperstones.

1 Exit the car park back to the road. Go RIGHT for a few metres and then go LEFT over a stile picking up a footpath and following it with a fence on the left to walk to the bottom left-hand corner of the field. Pass barns on the left and go through a small gate to exit the farmyard going straight ahead to follow the track, passing to the RIGHT of the farmhouse and passing another barn on the left. Go straight ahead through a gate/opening to follow the track for a few metres and then turn half LEFT to drop to the bottom of the sloping field to the fence and go RIGHT following it on the right, continuing to cross a bridge and a stile. Go over the next field to cross a little brook to the right of large tree and continue ahead to cross a stile near a gate to reach a lane. Go LEFT and descend the lane and when it bends sharp left, follow it to pass a cottage and at the end of this, at a hedge gap on the right go RIGHT over the stile on the footpath. Climb to cross another stile and continue climbing on the left of the field curving RIGHT and RIGHT again (but always keeping the fence left) to reach a stile. Cross, bear half LEFT to a marker post to go LEFT on a track through a felled forest area. Continue ahead as another track joins and stay on the track – which becomes more a path after a dip. After a marker post, the path descends gradually and odd marker posts keep you going right. Continue to reach a path junction with The Shropshire Way.

2 Go RIGHT along the track rising to pass through gates and continue uphill through rocky outcrops. As the ground levels out at a Shropshire Way marker post, leave the track going RIGHT to go half RIGHT at a second marker post and climb up to the ridge above to climb past two signs (keeping ahead each time), and reach a stile and gate. Cross, and leave the path to go LEFT following a sheep track for a while with the fence left. When this sheep track ends, turn RIGHT up the hillside over Nipstone Nature Reserve, veering LEFT to pick up a good path that will take you over the summit rocks. Continue on the path towards the obvious Nipstone Rock ahead, following the path to reach the rock. Take one of the easterly paths to head over the moor and pick up the good track of The Shropshire Way again near a gate and fence with a stile. Go LEFT to cross this stile, cross the track and take the track opposite towards the end of the plantation to pass through a kissing gate and enter the trees. Follow the path along the edge of them, passing through two fence gaps (one with a stile). Cross a stile after a gate on the right, still on The Shropshire Way and exit woods going over the field ahead on faint path, and go LEFT of hawthorn bushes to pass a footpath sign and telegraph post, staying ahead towards a gate in the hedge ahead. Pass through to reach a lane.

3 Cross the lane to go through a kissing gate picking up The Shropshire Way on the other side. Pass through another kissing gate to reach an information board and follow a good path uphill which develops into a wide track and climbs the broad heathery ridge end of The Stiperstones NNR. A path comes in from the left and you continue to climb steadily up to go LEFT at the next path junction heading towards Cranberry Rock above. Stay on the good path going LEFT of the rocks once you reach them, to curve RIGHT in front of the third and tallest outcrop to cross a boulder field and go LEFT on a fainter path to the right of rocks. At the outcrop end join a good path rising from the car park (not visible) below. *NOTE – there are paths meandering in all directions along the ridge so don't panic if you miss one – the* general direction is north and if you head that way the main ridge path will soon be found. Continue ahead after a path joins and stay RIGHT when it splits to head towards the RIGHT of the outcrop ahead, and drop to re-join the main course of The Shropshire Way, going RIGHT towards Manstone Rock, which has a trig point on the top. *NOTE – you need to be a competent scrambler with a head for heights to get to the trig.*

4 Return to main path and head north again. It is very rough at this point but nice and wide and easy to follow. Meander through the outcrops of the Devils Chair and then descend, continuing ahead when a path joins from left. Continue ahead towards Shepherds Rocks and, just before the next large outcrops, reach a good track at a distinct crossroads of paths. Here go RIGHT and descend in the direction of The Wrekin in the distance to reach a wall gap, stile and gate. Pass through to the field beyond going half RIGHT on a grass path to go right of a fence corner and pass through a gate in a fence and go half RIGHT to follow a grassy path over a field to reach a track below.

Map labels:
Shropshire Way
Devil's Chair
Stiperstones National Nature Reserve
Gatten Plantation
Manstone Rock
④
Cranberry Rock
To the A488
③
START
Knolls Farm
The Knolls
Nipstone Rock
Stiperstones
The Rock
②
⑤
①

5 Go RIGHT along this and leave it almost immediately as it bends left to go RIGHT on a footpath, cross a stream and go half RIGHT alongside the gorse hedge heading for trees ahead. Reach a stile and gate and pass through climbing uphill through trees. Rise to gates and a cattle grid and pass through, continuing to rise on a good track and keeping the fence left. Ignore any other paths or tracks and stay ahead on the main one continuing to pass a bench and an information point. Follow the good track ahead to bend LEFT and pass through a kissing gate and pick up the surfaced track beyond. Follow this to stay RIGHT as it splits to rise up and pass through a gate and re-enter the car park.

MYTTON DINGLE & GREEN HILL

DESCRIPTION Even though the Stiperstones Ridge is one of Shropshire's best known hill areas, there is a section of it at the northern end that is visited much less often than the more famous southerly parts of the region. The route described below starts at the pub in the village of stiperstones and climbs the wonderfully named, and atmospheric, Mytton Dingle to take in the summits of Oak Hill, Green Hill, The Castle Ring ancient hill fort and also includes an unnamed and very wild summit. The return is made down yet another valley, this one being the intriguingly named Perkins Beach. This is a rough and tumble outing with some steep climbs and great views. Save it for a day of clear weather as the way out and back to the unnamed top is over trackless ground and the going rough. 4¼ miles, 3 hours.

START There is a good car park by the Stiperstones Inn and village shop in the village of Stiperstones. The pub owners don't mind walkers using the parking area, but you must check before leaving your vehicle (01743 791237). SJ 363004.

DIRECTIONS Stiperstones village is east of the A488 south of Minsterley.

1 Leave the car park going RIGHT along the road passing the pub. Reach a junction on the right and go RIGHT, going LEFT of the phone box (signposted – 'Mytton Dingle') and rise steeply up the drive. Pass a house on the RIGHT continuing up the drive to a gate/stile. Pass through taking the track beyond and passing through more buildings and reach a gate by the last building. Go LEFT taking a path to the LEFT of a house. The track rises steadily through woodland to exit the trees and pass a Stiperstones notice board. Climb up Mytton Dingle passing spoil heaps. Further up the path climbs steeply veering half LEFT up the valley. At a low wooden barrier turn half LEFT to take a very steep path up to exit the valley at a low barrier.

2 Go LEFT, taking a narrow path around the head of valley following it over a minor top to descend to a col. As you reach the col go RIGHT on a narrow path rising to a good track at a T-junction. Go LEFT on this and stay on it climbing to the summit of Oak Hill. Continue to the ridge end for great views down to the village. Retrace steps back to the col and go LEFT, staying LEFT as the path splits, and follow the track passing over a minor bump and staying LEFT at a fork to descend (the path becomes vague) and cross earth work climbing up to the hill fort (Castle Ring). Re-trace your steps back to col.

3 Go LEFT climbing to a track with trees and a fence left. Here go RIGHT following a track to a crossroads with the barrier and head of Mytton Dingle (from your outbound route) to the right. Go LEFT steeply climbing to a good track at a T-junction. Go RIGHT on this for a hundred metres or so and choose a spot that looks less tangled than others and head LEFT and easterly over rough trackless ground, working a way to rocks and a cairn on the summit of the area above The Paddock. Re-trace your steps back to the good track going LEFT along it towards the main Stiperstones ridge. As an outcrop appears ahead go RIGHT on a track downhill, descending to a high level col with spoil heaps. Go straight over climbing up the ridge of Green Hill to the small cairn on the LEFT above Perkins Beach. Re-trace your steps to the col.

4 Go RIGHT on the faint grassy path which improves and descends Perkins Beach. Follow the path down the valley passing spoil heaps and odd buildings. The path descends to become a green lane and reach a gate/stile by sign. Pass through going RIGHT at a fork on a good track. Follow this to pass two houses on the left continuing to descend through more houses. Stay on the track (signposted 'village and pub') following it as it becomes surfaced to pass a footpath sign on the left and reaching the phone box again. Go LEFT past the pub and LEFT again back into the car park.

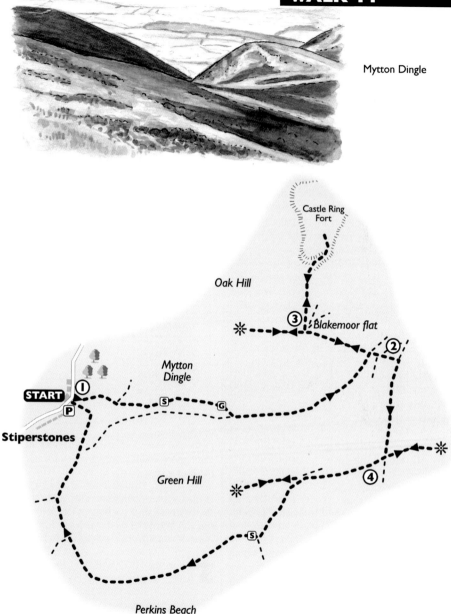

Mytton Dingle

Castle Ring Fort

Oak Hill

Blakemoor flat

Mytton Dingle

START

Stiperstones

Green Hill

Perkins Beach

A **giant red dragon** *and a giant green dragon fought a terrible battle over the county of Shropshire in the mists of time long ago. It was a battle witnessed in a dream by Merlin the fabled wizard of the court of Camelot. Neither could defeat the other and* *finally, locked together in their death throes, they fell to earth and formed the ridges of the Stiperstones and the Long Mynd as we see them today. From the air the two parallel ridges bear a strange resemblence to two fallen dragons – or perhaps it just depends*

BETCHCOTT HILLS & THE DARNFORD VALLEY

DESCRIPTION The area to the north and west of the Long Mynd is a lot less well known than the more famous hill country above Church Stretton. The Darnford Valley is a delightful area to go walking in with its own long distance path, The Darnford Way, winding along it, and the Betchcott Hills are wonderful hill walking country. A right of way follows the main ridge but it is a pity that you can't actually access the trig point on the top. This route follows the Golden Valley and climbs along the Betchcott Hills ridge to even higher ground beyond. A little lane walking follows. 7½ miles, 4 hours.

START Use the car park for the Horseshoe Inn at Bridges, but you must check at the pub before leaving your car (01588 650260). SO 393964.

DIRECTIONS Bridges is situated on minor roads west of the A49 at Church Stretton and south of Pontesbury on the A488

1 Leave the car park going LEFT and then RIGHT at the road junction, walking along the lane and passing the youth hostel (right). Reach a gate and stile on the LEFT before a bridge. Cross this stile picking up the footpath beside the brook on the right. Walk through the woods going half LEFT at a path junction near a bridge right. Cross the stile continuing with the brook right crossing a bridge into the woods. Walk through the trees finally rising to cross two stiles over a track and continue on the path crossing a stile and going half LEFT following the arrow to a finger post and continuing on the path with the brook to the right. Cross a stile going half LEFT to go LEFT of buildings rising past a finger post and going RIGHT of a quarry face. Climb steadily staying RIGHT by an arrow at a junction. At the next junction turn RIGHT crossing a stile. Cross a bridge

continuing on the path crossing some more bridges. Go LEFT at a path split to avoid boggy areas rejoining the main path further on. Cross several bridges and rise towards trees. Cross a stile continuing to descend towards farm buildings. Cross a stile near the buildings continuing to go LEFT rising up on a track to stay RIGHT at a path split walking to a stile by a gate.

2 Cross the stile going half RIGHT and descending trackless ground to cross two bridges, rising to go LEFT (by a post) following the path and climbing up Golden Valley. Climb up, crossing a stile and continuing past a marker post. Near the valley head stay LEFT, taking the fainter

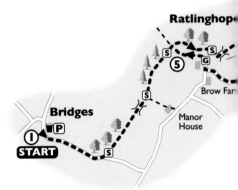

path and rising to pass through a kissing gate, going RIGHT on a surfaced track. Pass through a gate climbing the hill with a fence on the right. Pass through a gate in a field corner, keeping the fence right and following the footpath and passing below the summit trig (*no access to this*). Keep the fence to the right descending to a gate in the field corner.

3 Go to the RIGHT of the gate on a track which passes through a gate and climb up passing through a gap. Keep the fence to the left, climbing and passing through a gate and continuing towards trees, before passing through two gates and then climbing again with the fence to the left. Descend on a track to go to the RIGHT of a plantation, passing through a gate and curving LEFT and then going RIGHT at a fingerpost to climb the steep path to reach a road.

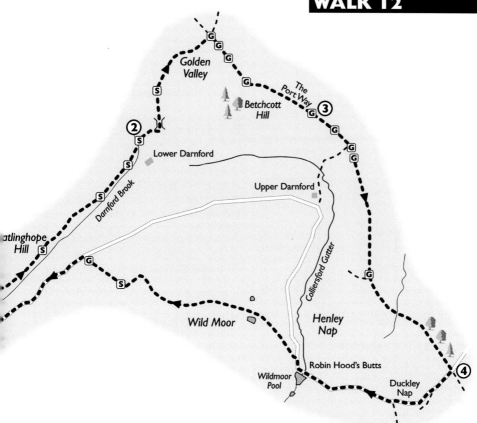

4 Go RIGHT on the road climbing over the moor and finally descending to go half LEFT by a finger post, after a pool on the left. Climb the track eventually levelling out and then descending steeply. At a split go LEFT on a fainter path descending to cross a stile, dropping down the field on a faint path and exiting onto a lane via a gate. Go LEFT following the lane for some distance until it bends left with a church on the right. Go RIGHT on an access track to pass through a gate descending to cross a bridge near a ford. Rise to join your outbound route near a stile left.

5 Go LEFT over the stile following your outbound route and crossing three stiles to exit to a lane. Go Right walking past the youth hostel and going LEFT and RIGHT to reach the car park again. *The Horseshoe Inn is also known affectionately as 'The Bridges' and is gaining popularity both with walkers and music lovers. Currently the music nights can number four each week, and combined with a meal it can make a really pleasant night out.*

WALK 13

A SHORT CIRCUIT OF STANYELD

DESCRIPTION Of all the 'batches' – hollows and valleys that cut deeply into the eastern side of The Long Mynd – The Carding Mill Valley is the tourist showpiece and justifiably the most popular and best known. There was actually a 'carding mill' here for hundreds of years, and it owed its existence to the constant stream of water the valley provided. This walk takes you to a hollow missed by most to visit the lonely summit of Stanyeld, with dramatic views back down to the valley floor. A return is made over the high level golf course and via a dramatic descent back to your car. At about 1½ miles it should take you no more than 1½ hours, but there is some steep climbing in the early stages.

START The Carding Mill Valley has numerous pay and display parking areas. This walk uses the first car park on the left as you drive into the valley. SO 446943.

DIRECTIONS Carding Mill is best reached from Church Stretton by turning off the A49 at the traffic lights into the town and driving to the top of the main street and going right. Follow this road and you will shortly see the Carding Mill Valley signposted via a left turn.

1 From the car park head north west down the Carding Mill Valley with the stream on the left. Just before a house ahead on the right and a bridge on the road ahead, leave the valley road and turn half RIGHT up the house approach track, veering RIGHT off it shortly to take a grass path heading into the gully ahead. A narrow path winds up the valley which soon starts closing in all around. Stay RIGHT when the valley splits and head up the RIGHT fork, following the path more steeply up towards the fence at the valley head above, and reaching it to the right of a gate.

2 Go RIGHT alongside the fence keeping it left and follow the path staying LEFT as it splits to go LEFT with the fence. Stay alongside the fence and just after it reaches it highest point, continue a short way to take a path RIGHT, which climbs to the unmarked summit of Stanyeld – *with awesome views down in The Carding Mill Valley far below.*

3 Re-trace your steps back to the fence and go LEFT following your outbound route to the valley head, going RIGHT through the gate to cross directly over the golf course (taking care) for a short way to reach a track. Go RIGHT on this following it to eventually descend and wind down the hillside to a T-junction of tracks facing a green of the golf course.

4 Here go RIGHT to follow the track to a gate and go RIGHT onto the track as directed by the yellow arrow. Continue on this by the golf course to curve RIGHT at a corner and reach a gate to the right of black buildings and a house. Pass through following the path to descend on it back into Carding Mill Valley, gradually at first and then more steeply to reach the valley road. Go RIGHT on this and walk back to your car.

WALK 14

THE NEW POOL HOLLOW RESERVOIR

This walk in the Carding Mill Valley follows the valley floor passing the Visitor Centre before undertaking a dramatic scramble over a rocky rib and visiting New Pool Hollow. A circuit of the reservoir is followed by a return down the hollow and back to your car. This route is 2 miles and you should allow yourself about 2 hours to avoid rushing it. *Avoid in wet conditions as the rock traversed is slippery.*

1 Leave the car park heading north-west up The Carding Mill Valley. Cross a bridge and continue to pass The Visitor Centre on the right side. Just past the houses yurn RIGHT over a bridge signposted 'footpath avoiding ford' and go LEFT with

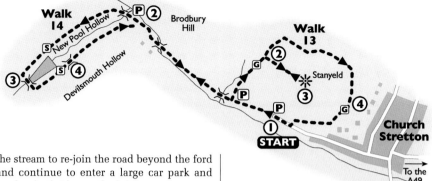

the stream to re-join the road beyond the ford and continue to enter a large car park and reach a footbridge on the left.

2 Go LEFT over the bridge stay RIGHT as the path splits. Take the good surfaced track. As the path curves right near a small reservoir on the left, leave it to go RIGHT up a grassy path to climb steeply to reach a rock outcrop above. From the base of the rocks follow the obvious way to scramble carefully up the rocks. Follow the worn way around the next outcrop, curving into a groove between outcrops to climb RIGHT up the right side rocks and at the top turn LEFT to pick up a good path that you follow towards the dam wall. Reach it at the right-hand end and cross a stile to follow the path along the right side, reaching a stone bridge on the left at the end of the reservoir, before a fence ahead.

3 Go LEFT over the bridge and follow the path LEFT crossing boardwalks. At the end of the final one go LEFT down steps to go RIGHT over a stile and then LEFT over a bridge crossing the reservoir outflow. Go RIGHT once over and follow the fence to the outflow to drop down steps to the base of the dam wall and a good path.

4 Take the path down New Pool Hollow to curve LEFT after two reservoirs on the right to reach the bridge from your outbound route. Cross it RIGHT into the car park going RIGHT and back down the road to go LEFT of the ford. Follow the path to go RIGHT over a bridge and then LEFT past the Visitor Centre and back to your car.

New Pool Hollow

HADDON HILL & THE UPPER CARDING MILL VALLEY

DESCRIPTION This route climbs from the top of the spur that rises facing New Pool Hollow and traverses the summit ridge of Haddon Hill. The actual summit is not visited, but you pass close enough to it to justifiably claim that you have been to the top! From Haddon Hill the route follows good tracks over the Long Mynd with awesome views all around, before returning to the start by dropping down the upper reaches of the narrow Carding Mill Valley. 3¼ energetic miles, allow 2½ hours.

START The Carding Mill Valley has numerous parking areas. They are pay and display and fairly expensive for a full day ticket. At weekends it gets quite packed. Use any of the very first car parks on the left as you drive into the valley. SO 446943

DIRECTIONS Carding Mill is best reached from Church Stretton by turning off the A49 at the traffic lights into the town and driving to the top of the main street and going right. Follow this road and you will shortly see the Carding Mill Valley signposted via a left turn.

I From the car park head north west down the Carding Mill Valley with the stream on the left. Continue on the road to pass the Visitor Centre and Tea Rooms passing through buildings to go RIGHT over a bridge, going LEFT on a footpath to avoid further road walking. Continue to cross a bridge to the right of a weir and reach two boulders where the path joins the road again. Here go half RIGHT taking the path towards the rocky rib of the ridge above (*be careful not to take the path fully right which will take you into the Batch*). Leave the path at the base of the ridge proper to work a way up the rocks sticking as closely as possible to the crest for the best views. A

path climbs the ridge to your left, but unless the weather is wet or the ground slippery, aim to stay on the crest as much as possible and work a way up the ridge. Near the top the ridge broadens and becomes grassier. Continue to go LEFT just before you reach a fence and gate with a golf course beyond. Drop down on the left of the fence and walk to the fence corner.

2 Carry on ahead climbing steeply up the slopes of Haddon Hill. Ignore turnings left and right as you climb and cross a good path. Climb up the wide grassy path between the fern. Stay RIGHT at a split near a grassy hollow and climb to a path T-junction with a traversing path. Go LEFT on this and take the second turning off it on the RIGHT at a crossroads. Climb the good wide path curving slightly RIGHT and continuing over the lower summit of the hill. Drop down to curve RIGHT and slightly LEFT to climb up and over the main summit of Haddon Hill. Continue to descend slightly, passing the head of the Batch, rising up again to go LEFT at a fork in the path. Continue to reach a T-junction with a good track

3 Go LEFT on this track across the Long Mynd, watching for a good path going left at a junction, and take this heading towards the upper reaches of the Carding Mill Valley. At a fork go RIGHT to walk a short way and join a good track (The Jack Mytton Way).

4 Go LEFT on this heading down the upper reaches of the valley on a good path. The scenery is very dramatic and the good path descends to a path junction and a ford where a valley (Light Spout Hollow) comes in right.

5 Cross the stream continuing ahead down the Carding Mill Valley with the stream on the left. Stay on the right hand side of the valley on a good path (avoiding higher ones that climb out of the valley) descending to a bridge which you cross

The Carding Mill Valley

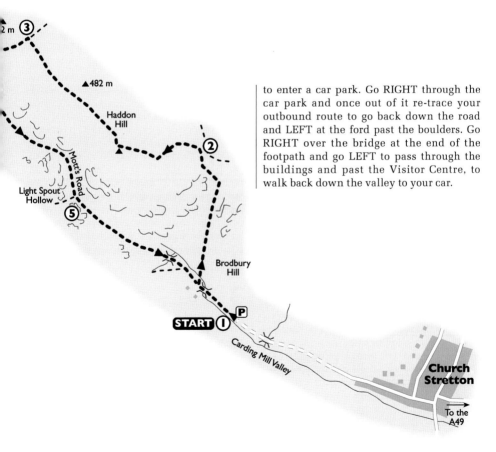

to enter a car park. Go RIGHT through the car park and once out of it re-trace your outbound route to go back down the road and LEFT at the ford past the boulders. Go RIGHT over the bridge at the end of the footpath and go LEFT to pass through the buildings and past the Visitor Centre, to walk back down the valley to your car.

NOVERS HILL & BODBURY HILL

DESCRIPTION The Long Mynd, west of the A49, is a magnificent upland of rolling hills and is crossed by a superb high level motor road. One of its many great attractions is the valleys that slice into the hillsides, giving access to hidden places and great routes onto the hills. The Batch Valley, the starting and finishing point for this route, is a narrow, straight valley that runs westwards and eventually curves to climb to the upper slopes of the surrounding hill country. This route climbs over the access land of two of the lesser known hills of the area, Novers Hill and Bodbury Hill. Both are worth climbing and the views are great throughout. There are also some pretty steep ascents and one (off Novers Hill) extremely steep descent. *Take care on the golf course!* 3 miles, 2 hours

START The Batch Valley has two parking areas, one near the entrance and one further on near the Youth Hostel. Both are free, but the road linking them is narrow and there is limited space to leave your car – so arrive early. SO 454954.

DIRECTIONS Enter All Stretton from the A49 and stay right and when the lane splits you come to a T-junction. Here you need to go RIGHT and then LEFT to follow a winding lane to the Batch Valley.

I From the car park at the entrance to The Batch Valley cross the bridge over the stream going RIGHT to pass the car park (now on the other side of the stream) and walk along with the stream to the right to turn back LEFT on a path just before a bench on the other side of the stream. Climb steeply above the car park again. The path develops into a good track. Just after the bridge in the car park below left, turn back RIGHT on a narrower path and climb steeply up Novers Hill to curve LEFT as the path splits. Go RIGHT (still uphill) just before a large tree. Follow the wide grass path climbing steeply. The angle eases higher up and just before an obvious dip ahead, curve RIGHT on a

narrower path to go RIGHT of the dip. Pick up a path over to the right, going LEFT along the edge of the hill with the valley below right. Follow this path to curve LEFT (staying on the edge) and climb to the bushes on the unmarked summit of the hill. Continue ahead in the same direction still following the edge to descend along a narrowing ridge to a rocky knoll. Go LEFT to pick a careful way down very steep slopes through the gorse using odd paths and sheep tracks going initially RIGHT of a small reservoir with railings before heading properly down. *TAKE CARE ON THIS SECTION AS IT IS VERY STEEP.* Aim for the road below and if you get it absolutely right you should arrive at a marker post just before it.

2 Go RIGHT along the road for a few metres to go LEFT before a telegraph pole, climbing a wide grassy path, with a fence on the left, to pass through a gate. Go straight ahead up the obvious gully following a good path and going to the LEFT of a groove when it appears. Cross a path near the top of the gully and continue to pass a warning sign for the golf course and continue to climb to reach a track and the golf course. Cross the track going half LEFT, passing a red topped marker post and walk over the course (with care) to pass through a gate in the fence. Take the path ahead and climb steeply up to the upper reaches of Bodbury Hill, again taking care. An alternative path curves right and then left from the gate to avoid the worst of the steepness. Either way you will arrive at an old earthworks on the summit and the actual top is to your left and is waymarked.

3 From the summit, cross the earthworks and head slightly east of north on trackless ground (towards The Lawley in the distance) to descend to a fence gap. Pass through, going to the RIGHT of a bench and walk over the course a few paces to reach a marker post to pick up the track and right of way. Go LEFT along it, continuing ahead at a pond on the left as the track becomes grassy. Curve LEFT to rise over the golf course on a good path and then descend to a gate in a fence at a valley head.

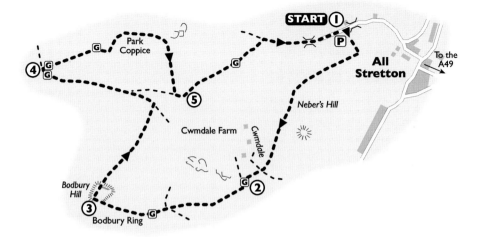

4 Pass through the gate going RIGHT and following the fence, with the valley below left. Reach another gate and pass through onto National Trust land and re-enter the golf course. *Church Stretton Golf Course is an 18 hole course and the oldest in Shropshire, having been open since 1898. It is at an altitude of 1,148ft (350 metres).* Follow the path along the rim of the valley, staying RIGHT when it splits, to leave the edge and follow the fainter path over the edge of the course passing blue and white marker posts. Descend to a gully, with the valley below left, and curve RIGHT to the valley head

5 Go LEFT at a path junction and LEFT again at the next junction to head on a good path down into the valley and towards the Batch Valley below. Descend to go LEFT of a gate and continue down on the good path to pass through another gate between fences, and continue between fences to eventually turn RIGHT and join a good track in The Batch Valley at a marker post. Go RIGHT along the track, with the brook to your left and cross the brook at a ford via a bridge on the left. Go RIGHT to pass to the LEFT of a house and follow the valley track back to your car.

Near Novers Hill

JONATHAN'S HOLLOW & GOGBATCH

DESCRIPTION This walk starts in the delightful Batch Valley and follows it to branch off into the wonderfully named Jonathan's Hollow. Following this onto the high ground of the Long Mynd, the route continues over Plush Hill to descend very steeply to Gogbatch. This route includes some steep ascents and descents, and the descent into Gogbatch would not be suitable in wet conditions or if the slopes were icy. That apart, this is a great walk for exploring the often ignored wild country of the northern Long Mynd. 5 miles, 3 hours.

START The Batch Valley has two parking areas, one near the entrance and one further on near the Youth Hostel. Both are free but the road linking them is narrow and there is limited space to leave your car so arrive early. SO 454954.

DIRECTIONS Enter All Stretton from the A49 and stay right when the lane splits. You then come to a T junction. Here you need to go RIGHT and then LEFT to follow a winding lane to the Batch Valley.

1 Walk west up the Batch Valley passing a house on the left and continuing past a 'No Unauthorised Vehicles' sign to cross a bridge near a ford. Go half RIGHT on the good track staying on it with the brook right to walk up the valley. Pass a cottage (The Batch) up to your left further up before reaching a path fork by a ford, with a gate left.

2 Take the RIGHT fork crossing the ford via a bridge, to follow the brook, now on your left. Pass a cottage on your right. Continue to cross a little bridge to continue up the narrowing valley. Continue to a crossroads, with a footpath going right and two valleys to the left, and continue ahead ascending Jonathan's Hollow. The valley narrows as the path climbs and the way ahead is obvious. Stay ahead at a path junction near a prominent tree and curve LEFT climbing more steeply. Ignore turnings left or right and finally reach a large crossroads by a ford on the left (with a solitary tree ahead). Go RIGHT uphill, staying LEFT at a split to pass over a small crossroads, rising up to go RIGHT on a track when it is reached. Follow this, descending towards a white house below. Further on, take the path cutting half LEFT to go LEFT of the white house down the left-hand side of the fence to reach a road.

3 Cross over the road taking the faint path to drop over a small earthwork, picking up the good track beyond and descending on it. Stay ahead at a crossroads on the track and, as it starts to rise up, take the faint path LEFT walking to the right of Gogbatch, which is below left. Stay RIGHT at an obvious split to rise up to go RIGHT of a grass bump into a grassy hollow. As the path curves right leave it to go LEFT for a short distance on trackless ground, picking up an obvious path ahead. Rise on this curving LEFT and passing RIGHT of another grassy bump to reach another bump. Climb over this taking a path through the fern beyond. Descend steeply (care is needed on this section) going RIGHT of a rocky knoll lower down and follow the narrowing path to drop to the road below. *The final descent on this section is very steep over rocks and moss and should be avoided if wet or icy.* Go RIGHT on the road continuing along Gogbatch to bear RIGHT to reach a house – 'The Oaks' – on the left.

4 Here go RIGHT steeply uphill (signposted 'Plush Hill'), going to the right of a copse. As the fence on your left bears left, leave the main path to go LEFT with the fence continuing ahead when the fence bends left again. Rise gently joining the main path again and going immediately half LEFT on a broad track going to the RIGHT of trees below to the left. Follow the path over heath land descending to stay LEFT at a split and descending to a gate by a cottage. Pass through this going LEFT of the cottage and following the track to eventually curve LEFT, by a white cottage, rising up to a footpath sign and a lane

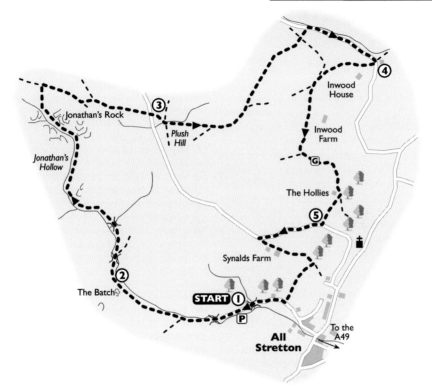

5 Go RIGHT on the lane climbing steeply up it to reach the entrance of a 'Bed & Breakfast' on your left and going LEFT here along the entrance drive and LEFT again immediately (unmarked) to take a track downhill, passing a bench on the left. Pass houses to take a track ahead descending on it to curve RIGHT, dropping steeply through woodland to reach houses. Pass a footpath sign to reach a lane. Go RIGHT along the lane following it to re-enter The Batch Valley and walk back to your car.

The Batch Valley

WALK 18

THE TOWNBROOK VALLEY

DESCRIPTION The Townbrook Valley is one of the narrowest of Shropshire's 'Batches' or 'Hollows'. From its start near a small reservoir, it winds a slender and atmospheric way up to the high hill country, exiting almost at the ever popular mountain road. It is a magical place. An ascent of the lovely summit of Yearlet is included on the return journey for the views and simply because you pass so close to it. The route concludes with a visit to an old chapel hidden deep by a pool in woodland – a truly peaceful place. 4¼ miles, 3 hours.

START From The Co-operative supermarket shoppers and 'Walkers Welcome' car park in the centre of Church Stretton. This is pay and display, and there are toilets. SO 454936.

DIRECTIONS From the traffic lights on the A49 at Church Stretton go either LEFT if coming from the south or RIGHT if coming from the north to drive up the main street over the railway bridge and turn LEFT once past the antique market into Easthope Road. A little along here you pass the toilets on the right. You then go RIGHT in front of the supermarket to go RIGHT into the car park.

1 Exit the car park towards the Co-op going RIGHT up Lion Meadow towards The Bucks Head public house and going RIGHT at the mini roundabout reached at the junction. Walk along the street crossing to go LEFT after a bank – this road is signposted for The Long Mynd (meaning 'long mountain'). Walk up the road and cross Church Street continuing ahead to carry on climbing up the road after the pavement ends. Take care as this is the approach to the mountain road and can be busy. Rise gently at first to eventually climb more steeply and pass through a gate by a cattle grid to reach a footpath LEFT.

2 Take the footpath LEFT (signposted 'Townbrook') along the track passing a

bench (right) and continue along the track, with woodland on the left, to finally descend on steeper ground to reach iron railings before a bridge with a reservoir to the right of it. Just before the railings, go RIGHT on a path signposted 'Townbrook'. Walk along the right-hand side of the reservoir beside the railings to enter the lower reaches of The Townbrook Valley. Follow the path, with a small brook on the left, and high hillsides on both sides, to wind a way up the valley ascending gently. After a decent sized scree run on the right curve slightly LEFT and begin to rise more steeply. The path becomes rougher and heads towards the end of the valley rising up above the stream on the left. Near the head of the valley the path winds a high level route along a shelf to eventually curve LEFT around the valley head to reach a finger post.

3 Here go ahead (ignoring The 'Pole Bank Walk' going right) continuing straight on and curving sharp LEFT. Just after the path curves left, and before a heathery mound ahead, go half RIGHT on a faint path to pass between two heathery mounds, and join a good track at a T-junction to the right of a rock outcrop. Go LEFT to pass to the RIGHT of the outcrop and climb the path ahead steeply up the hillside, ignoring any turnings off it in the initial stages. Reach a crossing of paths on the brow of the hill and go RIGHT to walk the short way to the cairn on the summit of Yearlet.

4 Re-trace your steps back to the crossing and go ahead descending gently. Go RIGHT when the path splits and follow a fainter path more steeply downhill towards the col and the good path below. As you descend the path becomes fainter, but don't worry if you lose it, the ground is not hard to walk over. Try and follow it all the way down and as you near the col, you pass over a path crossroads and go ahead to pick up the good track and right of way at the col. Go RIGHT and a little further on stay LEFT when it splits. Curve LEFT with The Townbrook Valley below left and follow the path through fern. As you descend it becomes wider and descends more steeply towards Church

The Townbrook Valley

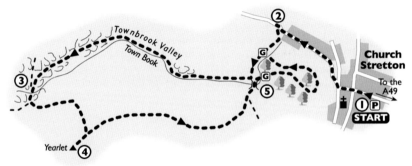

Stretton below. Descend towards trees and finally curve LEFT and continue with the trees below right. Ignore the first turning right and continue, staying RIGHT when the path splits again, descending to join a good path and going LEFT on it. Descend steeply down to cross a bridge by the reservoir on the left and just before the railings end, go RIGHT on a track with a stream right to descend to a kissing gate.

5 Pass through the kissing gate and enter the woodland. Follow path to a marker post staying LEFT when it splits near a bridge right. Keep the stream to the right and follow the path to a pool and an old ruined chapel near a marker post. Go LEFT at a path junction at the pool end and follow the steps uphill, zig-zagging up the hillside steeply to exit via a kissing gate and pick up your outbound route at a track. Go RIGHT and follow the track to the road, going RIGHT though the gate by the cattle grid and walking down the road back into Church Stretton. Go RIGHT at the road end and then LEFT at the mini roundabout to walk back to your car.

WALK 19

THE TOWNBROOK VALLEY HORSESHOE

DESCRIPTION The Townbrook Valley Horseshoe is one of the best 'rounds' in the region. Taking in the summits of Ashlet and Yearlet before working a moorland way around the head of the magnificent Townbrook Valley (see **Walk 18** for a route up the valley) and returning to Church Stretton over one of the few rocky ridges. All four summits visited are great viewpoints and well worth the effort of getting to. *Please note that the final descent is steep and can be slippery.* 4 miles, 3 hours.

START In Church Stretton. SO 450936.

DIRECTIONS Church Stretton is situated just off the A49. Drive up the main street over the railway bridge and turn LEFT at the T junction at the road end. Drive over the mini-roundabout and continue to go RIGHT near a church and follow this narrow minor road uphill curving RIGHT, LEFT and RIGHT again to reach the car park (free) on the right-hand side of the road.

Exit the car park, and go RIGHT downhill on a lane to curve slightly LEFT and join a rougher lane, which you follow to just before a house on the right. Here go RIGHT on the public footpath to walk along a narrow track and climb steps with an old wall on your right. Curve LEFT when the wall ends and continue steeply up steps through woodland with a fence to the right. At the top reach a stile, cross it and pick up a track heading RIGHT on it. Stay LEFT when it splits, almost immediately climbing uphill past old tree roots. As the path levels, and just before an old post, go LEFT taking a good path steeply uphill to curve back LEFT (as another path joins from the right) and follow the path climbing up the hillside. The path curves RIGHT as it continues climbing and is steep, wide and grassy. A little before the ridge is reached, look for a faint path going half LEFT – take this and climb diagonally across the hillside towards the summit of Ashlet. This path is intermittent and climbs towards the summit and ridge end. Stay RIGHT at any path splits and don't worry if you lose the path as the ground is easy to walk over. Pass a small rock step and, shortly after, as the path you are following curves left, go RIGHT climbing over trackless ground heading in the general direction of the summit and crossing a few minor bumps, to pick up the main ridge path and follow it LEFT to reach the unmarked summit of Ashlet.

2 Head north retracing your steps along the ridge path, staying LEFT on the higher path when the path splits. Follow this as it develops into a better path and curves LEFT around the hillside, continuing to re-join the good track of the original right of way which comes in from the right. Continue ahead up the hillside and, after a short distance, look for paths heading half left up the slopes of Yearlet. Take the LEFT of these paths heading towards a rock outcrop on the hillside above. Stay RIGHT when it splits and reach the outcrop to pass it on the LEFT-hand side. As the path vanishes above it continue uphill on the trackless ground to pick up the ridge path going LEFT on it to the cairn on the summit of Yearlet.

3 From the summit take a fainter path heading north-west and descend the hillside, curving slightly RIGHT and then LEFT to join a better path. Continue to descend to a col. Walk over the col, passing rocks, and take a fainter path beyond up the hill. This soon develops into a good track and rises to pass two marker posts. Continue to a third marker post and here, as the track splits, go RIGHT on a decent track to walk to the mountain road.

4 Go RIGHT along the road (taking care) and at the end of the third car park on the right take the track veering RIGHT leaving the road and heading towards the rocky top of Devils Mouth. Stay LEFT when this splits and follow it to a col (earthworks)

Stretton St Lawrence Church

just before the road. Continue ahead to climb a steep eroded path to the unmarked summit of Devils Mouth, and continue along the narrow ridge to drop down steeply to a broad grassy col. Continue on the grassy path to reach the unmarked summit of Burway Hill, the final top of the day. Continue ahead on the path staying RIGHT at a split, and when the path ends after heather, continue ahead on trackless ground towards Church Stretton. Shortly, trend RIGHT towards rocks (take care to locate them correctly) in the direction of a large white building below. Pass the rocks on the LEFT side to pick up a steep path below them. Follow this steeply down through the bracken – TAKE CARE AS IT IS VERY ROUGH AND SLIPPERY AND STEEP IN PLACES, AND IS NOT SUITABLE IN WET OR ICY CONDITIONS. Stay with the path to curve LEFT near the bottom and join a good track.

5 Go RIGHT, and descend to cross a bridge by a reservoir and follow the path ahead to climb up steeply on a path and rejoin your outbound route near the old post as the angle eases and the ground levels a bit. Descend to the stile on the left crossing it and descending the steps to curve RIGHT back to rough lane. Go LEFT following it to better lane which you follow back to the car park.

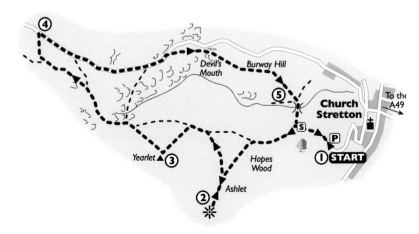

POLE BANK & ASHES HOLLOW

DESCRIPTION Pole Bank is the summit of the rolling hill country of The Long Mynd. The top reaches an altitude of 1,692ft and, if you save the route for a day with good visibility, a lot of the features indicated by the view finder can easily be picked out. Ashes Hollow is a classic way to ascend into the hills. The hollow is a deep valley that follows a babbling brook through steep hill country to the head of the valley and the source of the water. There is an exhilarating return back to Church Stretton using a lovely track. 6 miles, 3½ to 4 hours.

START There is roadside parking on the lane leading to the campsite near the Ragleth Pub in Little Stretton. Park alongside the brook and before Brook House and *please don't block the lane*. SO 442918.

DIRECTIONS Little Stretton is located a couple of miles south of Church Stretton and west of the A49 on the B5477. Parking is found by taking the second LEFT and continuing towards the camp site to go RIGHT at a T-junction near a left bend. If in doubt ask for directions to the campsite.

I Leave the parking area to walk up the lane, with the brook to the left and Brook House to the right. Cross the brook via a bridge at the fording point and go immediately RIGHT over a stile to enter the campsite and walk over the camping field, with the brook to the right heading for a gate on the far side to cross a stile in the right hand corner of the field. Follow a fence on your right to curve RIGHT around the field. As the valley narrows a path develops as you enter the lower reaches of Ashes Hollow. Continue next to the stream (right) to cross another stile and pass a rock face (left) to go RIGHT over a bridge. turn LEFT to go down the left-hand side of a house following the track towards the valley ahead. Walk with the brook to the left to head along the narrowing valley starting to gradually climb. Reach a footbridge and cross to the other side of brook to re-cross to the right bank a little further on. Continue to reach a stream coming in from the right and curve RIGHT to follow it, crossing it LEFT a bit further up to take the stoney path ahead uphill on the other side. Follow this path and go straight on when it splits to follow it high above the brook below left. Descend with the path to re-join the main path along the bottom of Ashes Hollow. The valley widens again but the path continues to climb. Stay RIGHT when a gully goes off to the left – at this point the valley begins to narrow again and the brook gets smaller. When the path splits, veer LEFT to cross the stream on stones to avoid an eroded area ahead. Re-cross the stream at bit further on to pick up the path on the right bank again. When the valley divides stay on the good path on the RIGHT and climb more steeply to curve LEFT, keeping the brook to the left and heading for the top of the valley. The valley continues to narrow and you exit it via a rock step to follow more level ground as the stream finally peters out to bear slightly RIGHT to reach the road.

2 Go LEFT on the road for a few metres, going RIGHT on a good track by a marker post. Follow the 'Pole Bank Walk', which is a good wide track, rising through heather to reach a path crossroads by a marker post and small wooden post. Go LEFT to climb to the trig and view finder on Pole Bank.

3 Leave summit in the same direction following the good track through the heather towards trees ahead. Descend to the road, going RIGHT along it. Continue on the road to pass the trees and a car park (both on the right) and a little further on reach a wide green track going off half LEFT.

4 Take this and go LEFT at a path junction along a wide track. Follow this track towards the flanks of Round Hill staying RIGHT when it splits to head for a marker post. Here bear LEFT to walk close to the summit area of the hill (a very rough walk south west on trackless ground will take you to the highest point if you really want to go). Descend down the other side of Round Hill dropping steeply to a col. Climb to curve

Pole Bank

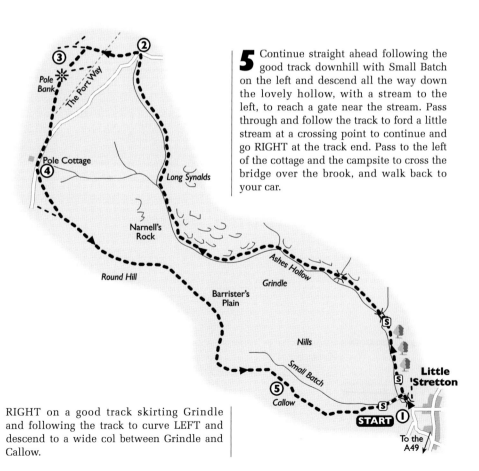

5 Continue straight ahead following the good track downhill with Small Batch on the left and descend all the way down the lovely hollow, with a stream to the left, to reach a gate near the stream. Pass through and follow the track to ford a little stream at a crossing point to continue and go RIGHT at the track end. Pass to the left of the cottage and the campsite to cross the bridge over the brook, and walk back to your car.

RIGHT on a good track skirting Grindle and following the track to curve LEFT and descend to a wide col between Grindle and Callow.

KEY TO THE MAPS

─────	Main road
━━━━━	Minor road
●▶●	Route
(1)	Walk instruction
– – –	Adjoining path
∿	Stream
G	Gate
S	Stile
△	Summit
🌲🌳	Woods
🍺	Pub
P	Parking

THE COUNTRY CODE

- Be safe – plan ahead and follow any signs

- Leave gates and property as you find them

- Protect plants and animals, and take your litter home

- Keep dogs under close control

- Consider other people

About the author, Steve Goodier...

Steve is a life-long outdoor enthusiast who has walked and climbed all over the United Kingdom and in many other parts of the world. He is a freelance writer based in Cheshire who produces regular routes for the likes of Country Walking Magazine as well as Walking Wales and Cumbria Magazine. A family man with two growing children, he spends as much of his spare time as he can camping and walking in our National Parks and mountain regions with the Lake District and Scotland being his personal favourites.

Published by
Kittiwake Books Limited
3 Glantwymyn Village Workshops,
Glantwymyn, Machynlleth, Montgomeryshire
SY20 8LY

© Text & map research: Steve Goodier 2010
© Maps (from ooc base): Kittiwake 2010
© Illustrations: Morag Perrott 2010

Cover photographs: *Main:* Stiperstones.
Inset: Towards Caer Caradoc. Steve Goodier.

Care has been taken to be accurate. However neither the author nor the publisher can accept responsibility for any errors which may appear, or their consequences. If you are in doubt about any access, check before you proceed.

Printed by Mixam, UK.

ISBN: 978 1 902302 82 9